KOBE BRYANT

THE INSPIRATIONAL STORY OF GRIT AND PERSEVERANCE

This book belongs to

_____

CONTENTS

CHAPTER 1

The Young Mamba

Once upon a time in a city called Philadelphia, there was a young boy who had a dream. This boy's name was Kobe Bryant. Kobe was born in Philadelphia, Pennsylvania on August 23, 1978. He was the son of Joe and Pam Bryant, both of whom were talented athletes. In fact, his dad, Joe "Jellybean" Bryant, played in the NBA, so you could say that basketball was in Kobe's genes.

But Kobe's love for the game went beyond just his family's influence. From an early age, he was captivated by the sound of a bouncing basketball, the squeak of sneakers on the hardwood, and the swish of the net.

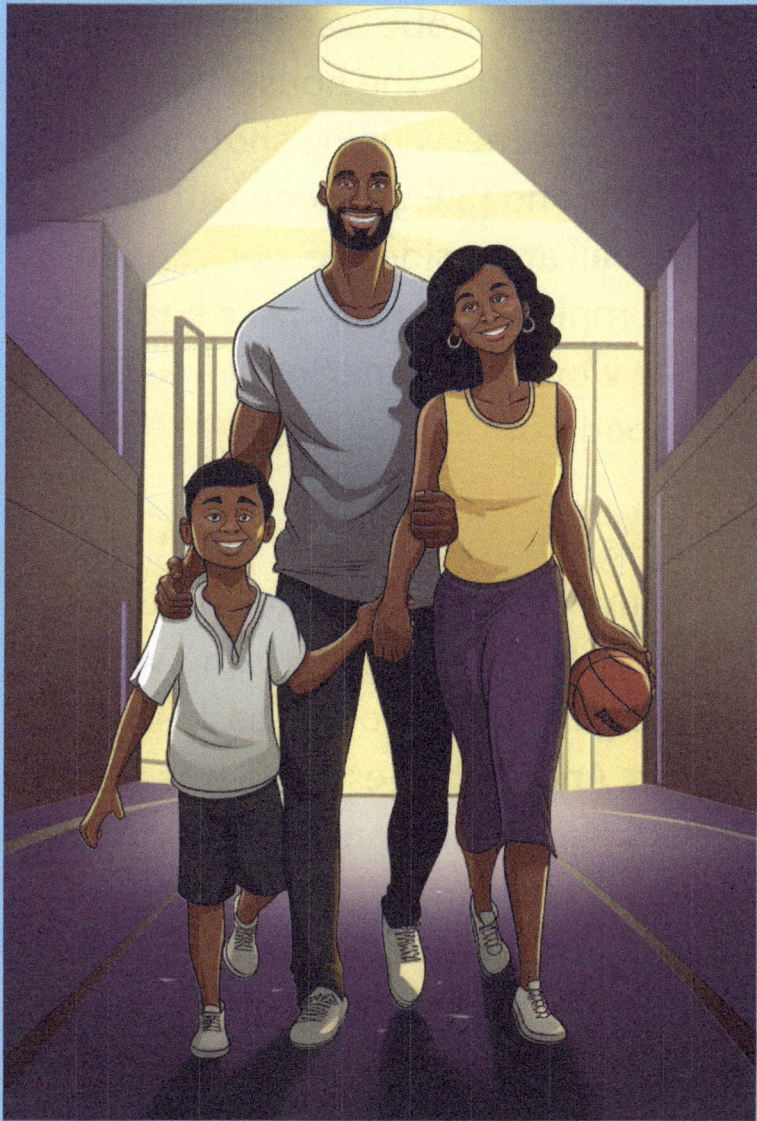

Even before he was old enough to play on a real team, Kobe was dribbling a basketball around the house, making imaginary game-winning shots in the driveway, and falling asleep with a basketball at his side. He would pretend the crumpled-up paper was a basketball, and he would take imaginary free throws in his bedroom.

Kobe's love for the game didn't end on the court. He spent countless hours watching basketball games on TV, studying the moves of his basketball heroes. And his biggest hero was a man named Michael Jordan. Kobe had posters of Michael Jordan on his bedroom walls, and he would watch his games over and over again, trying to learn all of MJ's amazing moves.

Kobe's family moved to Italy when he was just six years old because his dad was playing professional basketball there. In Italy, he fell in love with the sport even more. He would spend hours playing on the local basketball courts, practicing his skills and shooting hoops until the sun went down.

He had no idea that he would one day become one of the greatest basketball players in the world. But for the time being, he was just a little kid with a basketball and a dream, ready to take his first steps toward greatness.

And so, with a hoop in his heart and a basketball in his hand, Kobe Bryant's incredible journey began.

CHAPTER 2

High School Phenom

Kobe's basketball journey took an exciting turn when he entered high school at Lower Merion in Ardmore, Pennsylvania. It was here that he began to make a name for himself as a true basketball prodigy.

As a young teenager, Kobe joined the Lower Merion Aces basketball team, and it didn't take long for everyone to see that he was something special. He stood out with his incredible skills, determination, and a work ethic that was beyond his years. Kobe was more than simply a player; he was a high school star on the rise.

In his freshman year, Kobe's talent started to shine through. He played with the heart of a lion, and fans came to watch him play in packed gyms. He led his team to victory after victory, and his name began to spread like wildfire through the basketball community.

One of the most remarkable moments of Kobe's high school career was when the Lower Merion Aces won the state championship in 1996. It was a huge achievement for the team, and Kobe was a big part of it. He scored an incredible 31 points in that championship game, and it was a sign of the greatness that lay ahead.

Kobe continued to set records and earn awards during his high school years. He became the all-time leading scorer in the history of the school, a record that still stands today. His hard work, dedication, and his love for the game were paying off in a big way.

As Kobe's reputation grew, so did the attention from college basketball teams. Many colleges wanted him to play for their teams after he graduated from high school. But Kobe had other plans. He had dreamed of playing in the NBA since he was a little boy, and he was determined to make that dream come true.

In a bold move, Kobe made the decision to enter the NBA draft directly from high school. This was a rare and courageous choice, as most players went to college before entering the NBA. But Kobe believed in himself and his abilities, and he was ready to take on the challenge.

The world was about to witness the next step in Kobe's incredible journey, as he prepared to face the best basketball players in the world. High school was just the beginning; the young phenom was destined for even greater heights on the basketball court.

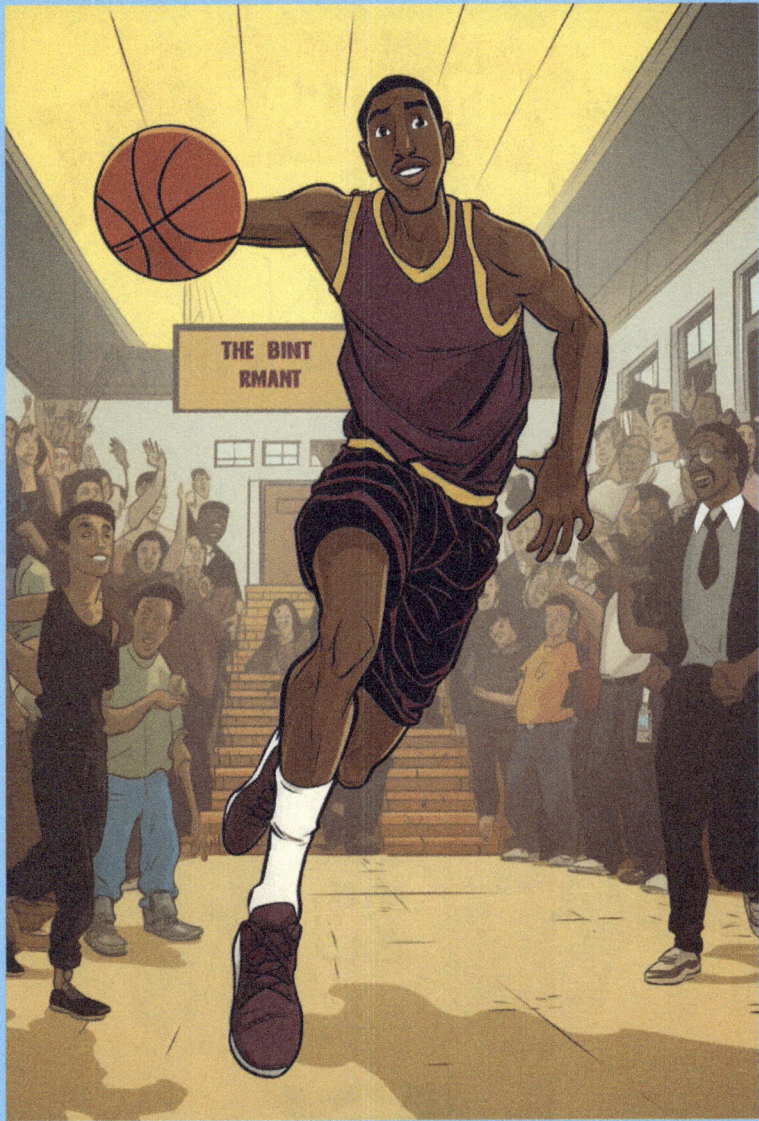

CHAPTER 3

The NBA Journey Begins

It was a day that Kobe had been dreaming of for as long as he could remember – the day he would step onto the big stage of the NBA. The moment he had been working so hard for had arrived, and it all started on a special day called "draft day".

Draft day is when the NBA teams choose new players to join their rosters. It's like a big basketball party where the best young talents from around the world hope to hear their names called.

On the day of the 1996 NBA Draft, Kobe Bryant was just 17 years old. He was excited and nervous, not knowing which team would pick him. But deep down, he had a feeling that something amazing was about to happen.

When the time came, the Charlotte Hornets selected Kobe with the 13th pick in the first round. However, Kobe was soon traded to the Los Angeles Lakers. He was headed to the City of Angels, where he would wear the purple and gold and play for one of the most famous and successful teams in NBA history.

Joining the Lakers was a dream come true for Kobe. He was going to play for a team that had legendary players like Magic Johnson and Kareem Abdul-Jabbar. But he knew that living up to the Lakers' rich history and winning championships would not be easy.

Kobe faced many challenges during his first year in the NBA. He was one of the youngest players in the league, and he had to adapt to the faster pace and stronger opponents. But Kobe was determined to prove himself.

He practiced tirelessly, both on and off the court, working on his skills and building his strength. He learned from his teammates and coaches and always asked questions to become a better player. His relentless work ethic was already a part of his "Mamba Mentality".

As the season went on, Kobe's talent began to shine through. He demonstrated to the rest of the world that he was a force to be reckoned with. Fans and teammates started to see his incredible skills, his fearless attitude, and his desire to win.

Kobe's journey in the NBA had just begun, and it was already filled with excitement and promise. The young rookie was ready to take on the world of professional basketball and prove that he belonged among the best.

CHAPTER 4

Shaq and the Three-Peat

Kobe's journey in the NBA took an exciting turn when he teamed up with one of the most dominant and charismatic players the league had ever seen – Shaquille O'Neal. Together, they formed a dynamic duo that would go on to achieve something truly special.

Shaquille O'Neal, often called "Shaq," was a giant on the basketball court. Standing at 7 feet 1 inch tall and weighing more than 300 pounds, he was a force to be reckoned with. Kobe, on the other hand, was quick, agile, and had incredible skills. When these two superstars joined forces, they became a basketball powerhouse.

The combination of Shaq's size and strength and Kobe's skill and speed was a recipe for success. The Lakers were a team to be feared. They played with passion and intensity, and fans across the country couldn't wait to see what they would do next.

In the early 2000s, the Lakers went on an incredible journey, winning three consecutive NBA championships in 2000, 2001, and 2002. This was a remarkable achievement, and Kobe played a vital role in each of these championships. His scoring ability, defensive prowess, and clutch performances in big moments were the keys to the Lakers' success.

The Lakers' three-peat was a historic feat, and Kobe and Shaq became basketball legends. They proved that when two great players come together as a team, they can achieve amazing things. The Lakers were the kings of the basketball world, and Kobe was on top of the world.

During this time, Kobe's nickname "Black Mamba" started to gain popularity. The Black Mamba is a type of snake known for its speed, agility, and deadly strikes. Kobe's friends gave him this nickname because of his on-court skills and his ability to strike fear into his opponents, just like the snake. The "Black Mamba" became an alter ego for Kobe, and it represented his fierce determination and competitive spirit.

CHAPTER 5

Trials and Triumphs

Life is not always a smooth path, even for heroes like Kobe Bryant. As Kobe continued his basketball journey, he faced personal and team challenges that tested his determination and character.

One of the biggest challenges came in the form of injuries. Kobe, like all athletes, had to deal with injuries during his career. In 2003, he suffered a major shoulder injury that kept him out of the game for a while. It was a tough time for Kobe, as he couldn't do what he loved most – play basketball. But he didn't give up. Instead, he worked hard to recover and get back on the court stronger than ever.

Another challenge came from critics and doubters who questioned whether Kobe could lead a team to victory without Shaquille O'Neal. Kobe was determined to prove them wrong. Shaquille O'Neal was traded away after the Lakers lost the 2004 NBA Finals. Kobe had to step up and become the leader who would carry the team on his shoulders. He embraced the challenge and became an even better player. He worked on his leadership skills and continued to inspire his teammates.

In 2008, Kobe's hard work paid off when he was named the league MVP (Most Valuable Player). This was a huge honor and a testament to his skills and dedication. But Kobe's ultimate goal was not just personal awards; it was winning championships.

In 2009 and 2010, Kobe led the Lakers to back-to-back NBA championships. He was the heart and soul of the team. His leadership and performance were crucial to their success. In both of those championship series, he was named the NBA Finals MVP, which is an award given to the best player in the championship round.

The Lakers' victories in 2009 and 2010 were a return to glory for the team, and Kobe was a major part of their triumph. He had overcome challenges, taken on new responsibilities, and continued to chase his dreams with unwavering determination.

CHAPTER 6

International Career

While Kobe Bryant was a basketball superstar in the NBA, he also had the opportunity to represent his country on the international stage. Playing for the USA national basketball team was a great honor for Kobe, and he made significant contributions to Team USA.

Playing for Team USA was a source of immense pride for Kobe. He knew he was not just representing himself but his country as well. He wore the red, white, and blue with honor and carried the spirit of the United States with him on the court.

49

Kobe's journey with the national team began with the 2008 Summer Olympics in Beijing, China. He was part of a "Dream Team" that included some of the best players in the NBA. The team was determined to bring home the gold medal, and they did just that, dominating their opponents to win the championship.

Kobe's incredible skills and competitive spirit were on full display during the Olympics. He was a key player, scoring important points, making crucial assists, and playing tough defense. His leadership and performance helped lead the team to victory, and he was a vital part of the "Redeem Team," as they were called, because they redeemed the gold medal that the USA had lost in the previous Olympics.

Kobe's international success didn't stop there. He went on to represent the USA in the 2012 London Olympics, where they once again won the gold medal. Kobe's dedication to his country and his ability to perform on the global stage solidified his status as one of the all-time basketball greats.

Kobe's international career was a testament to his versatility as a player and his ability to excel at the highest level of competition, whether in the NBA or on the world stage. He showed that his skills and the "Mamba Mentality" transcended borders and inspired people around the world.

CHAPTER 7

Beyond Basketball

Kobe Bryant's life was not just about basketball; he had a big heart and a deep commitment to making the world a better place.

One of the ways Kobe gave back to the community was through his charity work. He knew that there were people in need, and he wanted to help in any way he could. He started the Kobe and Vanessa Bryant Family Foundation to support important causes like education, health, and youth initiatives. He donated millions of dollars to help those in need and inspired others to do the same.

Kobe also had a creative side. He had a love for storytelling, and he expressed it in many ways. One of his most notable projects was the short film "Dear Basketball". This film was a heartfelt letter to the sport he loved so much. It was a beautiful and emotional tribute to his basketball career and his love for the game.

"Dear Basketball" went on to win an Academy Award (an Oscar) for Best Animated Short Film in 2018. Kobe was not just a basketball champion; he was an Oscar winner too, and this achievement showcased his talent beyond the court.

In 2016, after 20 incredible seasons in the NBA, Kobe made the difficult decision to retire from professional basketball. It was a bittersweet moment for his fans around the world. They knew they would miss seeing him on the court, but they also understood that Kobe had given his all to the game.

During his retirement, Kobe continued to work on various projects and initiatives. He published books, including "The Wizenard Series" to inspire young readers with the power of storytelling. He also stayed active in the sports world, supporting athletes and helping them achieve their best.

CHAPTER 8

Family and Legacy

Behind every great athlete, there is often a loving and supportive family. Kobe Bryant was no exception. He had a beautiful family that meant the world to him.

Kobe's wife, Vanessa, was his high school sweetheart. They fell in love and got married in 2001. They had four daughters together. Kobe was a loving husband and a devoted father.

Kobe's family was a source of strength and inspiration for him. They were by his side during his basketball career, cheering for him at games, and celebrating his victories. They were also there for him when he faced challenges and setbacks, providing support and encouragement.

After his retirement from professional basketball, Kobe didn't slow down. He continued to be involved in various projects and endeavors. He stayed connected to the world of sports, supporting and mentoring young athletes. He also ventured into the world of business, investing in technology and entertainment companies. His ambition and drive extended to all aspects of his life.

One of his most notable post-retirement projects was the creation of the "Mamba Sports Academy", a facility that aimed to help athletes of all ages and abilities reach their full potential. Kobe believed in giving back to the world of sports and sharing his knowledge with the next generation of athletes.

Tragically, in 2020, Kobe and his daughter Gianna, along with seven others, were involved in a helicopter crash that took their lives. The world mourned the loss of this basketball legend, but his legacy continued to live on. People from all around the world celebrated Kobe's life and the impact he had on so many.

Kobe's family and his legacy served as a reminder of the importance of pursuing your dreams, loving your family, and making a positive impact in the world. His story continued to inspire and motivate others, ensuring that his name would never be forgotten.

CHAPTER 9

Mamba Mentality

Kobe Bryant was known not just for his incredible talent on the basketball court but also for his unwavering work ethic and commitment to excellence. These qualities were at the core of what he called the "Mamba Mentality."

The "Mamba Mentality" was Kobe's secret weapon, his recipe for success. It meant being the best you could be, working harder than anyone else, and never giving up, no matter what. This mentality was about pushing yourself to the limit and then pushing a little more.

Kobe's journey to develop the "Mamba Mentality" began early in his life. He understood that to become great, he needed to put in hours and hours of practice. He would wake up early in the morning to shoot hoops, even before school. After school, he would be back on the court, perfecting his moves and honing his skills.

Kobe's work ethic was legendary. He didn't just practice during the regular season; he practiced year-round. Even on holidays and weekends, he would be in the gym, refining his game. He would spend hours studying game footage, looking for ways to improve. It was said that he often practiced until his hands bled, that's how committed he was to his craft.

One story that perfectly captured the "Mamba Mentality" was when Kobe injured his Achilles tendon during a game. Most players would have been sidelined for months, but not Kobe. He stayed in the game, made his free throws, and then walked off the court on his own. It was an incredible display of his determination and toughness.

Kobe's "Mamba Mentality" wasn't just about basketball; it was about life. He believed that the same dedication and hard work that had made him a great basketball player could be applied to any area of life. Whether it was business, art, or any other endeavor, he encouraged people to adopt the "Mamba Mentality."

"Great things come from hard work and perseverance," he often said. "No excuses." This was the essence of his philosophy, and he intended to share it with the rest of the world.

Kobe's journey was a living example of the "Mamba Mentality." He showed that with relentless dedication, you could achieve greatness, no matter where you started. His legacy was not just about basketball but about inspiring others to adopt the same mentality and chase their dreams with all their heart and soul.

Kobe's "Mamba Mentality" would continue to inspire people for generations to come, a legacy that extended far beyond the basketball court.

THE END

Made in the USA
Las Vegas, NV
03 October 2024